A NOTE TO PARENTS

David and Goliath is probably a story from your own childhood; perhaps the courage of David attracted you to the tale. Today's children see violence at every turn of the television knob. Rather than dwelling on the violence in this story, focus on the person of David.

In all likelihood, David was a teenager responsible for taking care of sheep alone after his bar mitzvah at age thirteen. Young children enjoy looking up to youths as role models. Talk about the earlier part of David's life. Point out how David helped his father and played music that made King Saul feel better. Encourage your child to think of ways that he or she can be helpful, like David.

You might also talk about how David must have practiced using his sling so that he could protect the sheep. David knew that God would help him since he had practiced. Talk about special things that your child has learned to do, and thank God for those things.

— *Delia Halverson*

Delia Halverson is the consultant for
Family Time Bible Stories. An interdenominational lecturer
on religious education, she has written nine books,
including *How Do Our Children Grow?*

Scripture sources: **1 Samuel 16:14-17:49**

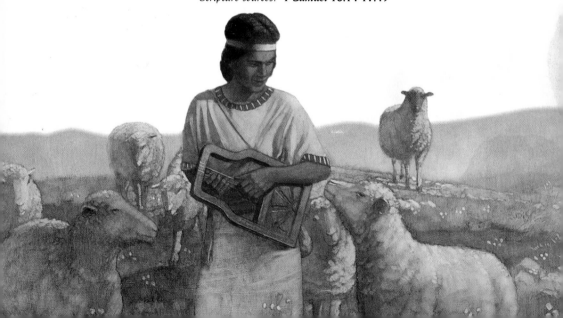

FAMILY TIME
BIBLE
STORIES

DAVID AND GOLIATH

Retold by Andrew Gutelle

Illustrated by Bill Farnsworth

ALEXANDRIA, VIRGINIA

David was a boy who lived a long, long time ago in the city of Bethlehem.
He was the youngest--and smallest--of eight brothers. It was David who

looked after his father's sheep. When he was not working, he played
music on his lyre. The people of Bethlehem said it was beautiful music.

One morning, as his sheep searched for
sweet bits of grass, David saw a man
coming up the road. What could this
stranger want?

"I bring greetings from King Saul of
Israel," said the man. "Our king's heart is
filled with sadness. He asks you to come
and play music to cheer him."

That day David set out on his father's donkey. He rode to the home of the king.

King Saul watched as he strummed the strings of his lyre. He listened as the boy sang. Then, finally, the king smiled.

"Your music brightens my home," said the king happily. He asked David to stay with him. The boy lived with King Saul for many months, soothing him with music.

Then, one day, a messenger came. An
army of Philistines was marching toward
the land of Israel. King Saul left to lead
his soldiers into battle. He sent young
David home to his father.

Three of David's broth-
ers had joined Saul's
army. David's father
worried about them.
One morning, he called
his youngest son.

"David, take this
bread and cheese to
your brothers," said his
father. "See that they
are well."

When David arrived, he saw the two armies facing each other across a wide valley. In the middle of the valley stood David's brothers with some other soldiers. They were looking at a giant man in glittering armor.

He was the biggest person anyone had ever seen.

"The armies do not need to fight," roared the giant. "Two people can settle this. Send out your best warrior, and I, Goliath, will defeat him!"

Nobody dared to fight Goliath—nobody except David. He hurried to see the king.

"You are just a boy. You have no chance against that monster of a man," said King Saul. "How can you possibly defeat him?"

"When a lion or bear used to come after my sheep," replied David, "I would strike it down with a stone from my sling. God, who protected me from the paw of the lion and the bear, will save me from the hand of Goliath."

King Saul could not argue with the boy's
faith. He gave David the king's own suit of
armor. It was so heavy the boy could barely
stand up. Saul's long sword dragged against
the ground.

"I cannot walk with these," said David
to King Saul. He took off the armor and put
on his own simple clothes.

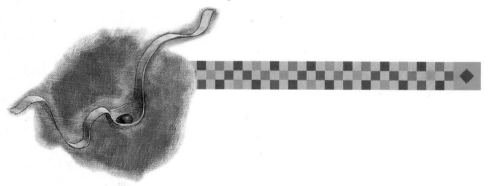

David took his sling
and went to meet
Goliath. Along the way
he stopped by a
stream. Reaching into
the cool water, he
picked up five smooth
stones. He dried each
one and put them all in
his leather pouch.

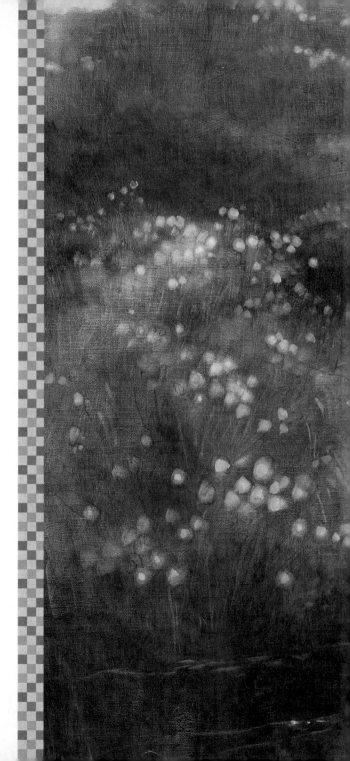

In the valley, Goliath was waiting. The armies stood watching. Slowly, David stepped forward from the soldiers. He was holding his sling.

When Goliath saw him, he laughed so hard that his armor rattled. "Am I a dog," he shouted to David, "that you come to me with sticks?"

David reached into his pouch and took out one stone. He placed it in his sling and spun it round and round.

With all his might, David let go and sent the stone whistling through the air. It struck Goliath in the forehead. For an instant, the giant stood silently. Then he came crashing to the ground.

David ran forward. He picked up Goliath's
sword and held it high above his head.
The soldiers in Goliath's army turned and
ran away, chased by the soldiers of Israel.

And David? He smiled. He knew that
God did not care who was big, or who had
the most armor. God was with him
because he had trusted God.

TIME-LIFE KIDS™
Staff for FAMILY TIME BIBLE STORIES

Managing Editor:	Patricia Daniels
Art Director:	Susan K. White
Publishing Associate:	Marike van der Veen
Editorial Assistant:	Mary M. Saxton
Senior Copyeditor:	Colette Stockum
Production Manager:	Marlene Zack
Quality Assurance Manager:	Miriam Newton

First printing. Printed in U.S.A.   Published simultaneously in Canada.

Time Life Inc. is a wholly owned subsidiary of THE TIME INC. BOOK COMPANY.
TIME-LIFE is a trademark of Time Warner Inc. U.S.A.
School and library distribution by Time-Life Education,
P.O. Box 85026, Richmond, VA 23285-5026.
For subscription information, call 1-800-621-7026.

Library of Congress Cataloging-in-Publication Data

Gutelle, Andrew. David and Goliath / retold by Andrew Gutelle; illustrated by Bill Farnsworth. p. cm. — (Family time Bible stories) Summary: Retells the story of the shepherd boy who relies on his faith and defeats the Philistine warrior who has led an army against Israel's King Saul.
ISBN 0-7835-4630-0 1. Bible stories, English—O.T. Samuel, 1st. 2. David, King of Israel—Juvenile literature. 3. Goliath (Biblical giant)—Juvenile literature. 4. Bible. O.T. —Biography—Juvenile literature. [1. David, King of Israel. 2. Goliath (Biblical giant) 3. Bible stories—O.T.] I. Farnsworth, Bill, ill. II. Title. III. Series.
BS580.D3G87 1996   96-538
222'.4309505— dc20   CIP
                                                     AC